FOR: _____

FROM: _____

*May the Lord make your love
increase and overflow for each other.*

~1 THESSALONIANS 3:12

Requests for information should be addressed to:
    Inspirio, the Gift Group of Zondervan
    Grand Rapids, Michigan 49530

Associate Editor: Molly Detweiler
Compiler: Pat Matuszak
Creative Manager: Patricia Matthews
Art and Design: Koechel Peterson & Associates, Mpls, MN

Printed in China
00 01 02 /HK/ 4 3 2 1

Love is patient love is kind

always pr

usts alway

rsevere L

nd now the

ith hope and love But

eatest of these is love Lo

tient love is kind It al

otects always trusts alu

TO LOVE & TO CHERISH

MEDITATIONS *for* COUPLES

inspirio
The gift group of Zondervan

"I LOVE YOU."

Three simple words are so critical to marriage.
We take these tender words for granted sometimes, but
we have never known anyone who got tired of hearing
"I love you" ... before leaving the house in the morning ... after
a quick message on the answering machine ...
while working in the garden ... before dozing off in bed.
These little words are like vitamins to a marriage.
We have over 600,000 words in the English language
and more synonyms per word than are found in any other language. However, we have only one word with which to express
all the various shadings of love.

-LES & LESLIE PARROTT

And wilt thou have me fashion into speech
The love I bear thee, finding words enough,
And hold the torch out, while the winds are rough,
Between our faces, to cast light upon each?

I drop it at thy feet. I cannot teach
My hand to hold my spirit so far off
From myself... me... that I should bring thee proof,
In words of love hid in me ... out of reach.

-ELIZABETH BARRETT BROWNING,
SONNETS FROM THE PORTUGUESE, XIII

If I speak in the tongues of men and of angels, but have not love, I am only a resounding gong or a clanging cymbal. If I have the gift of prophecy and can fathom all mysteries and all knowledge, and if I have a faith that can move mountains, but have not love, I am nothing. If I give all I possess to the poor and surrender my body to the flames, but have not love, I gain nothing.

Love is patient, love is kind. It does not envy, it does not boast, it is not proud. It is not rude, it is not self-seeking, it is not easily angered, it keeps no record of wrongs. Love ... rejoices with the truth. It always protects, always trusts, always hopes, always perseveres.

Love never fails.

-1 Corinthians 13:1-8

CHEERS

Some days I need a person to be the Bible in shoe leather for me. I need to see Jesus in someone. Often, that "someone" is my husband.

Marriage provides us with the unique opportunity to "be" Jesus for our mate in the lowest of lows and the highest of highs in life. Larry has been a friend who has ridden the waves with me as they have crashed into the shore—and he's been there with me when the waves have peacefully lapped the sand. Husbands and wives do that for each other. They show themselves friendly. Are you your mate's cheerleader? We need each other!

-RACHAEL CRABB

BANKING ON LOVE

We make deposits into each other's emotional bank accounts by meeting our partner's needs for deep listening, support, communication, intimacy, time together, and kindness. For example, when the husband wakes his wife with a lingering hug, a cup of coffee, and the newspaper, makes the bed, takes out the garbage, folds his and her clothes, and calls her parents, he makes deposits into her emotional bank account. When the wife surprises her husband with a new novel, welcomes him home with a kiss, asks him about the big project at work, prepares a favorite meal, and orders him to the family room to watch Saturday's big game, she makes deposits into his bank account.

One secret of a marriage made of two-part harmony is to fill each other's emotional bank account to overflowing, to make so many deposits that a vast reserve of trust, love, caring, affection, and intimacy shows up on the balance sheet. Then the assets will far exceed liabilities. The net worth of the marriage will exceed both of your expectations. You will have made each other wealthy in love, abundant in intimacy, and overflowing in trust.

-PATRICK MORLEY

Heavenly Father, sometimes we make so many withdrawals from each other's emotional bank accounts that our relationship is overdrawn. Lord, help us to make deposits to each other of love, caring, faith, patience, trust, help, time, deep listening, and companionship. Amen.

Above all, love each other deeply, because
love covers over a multitude of sins.

-1 PETER 4:8

AS WE HAVE OPPORTUNITY, LET US DO
GOOD TO ALL PEOPLE,
ESPECIALLY TO THOSE WHO BELONG TO
THE FAMILY OF BELIEVERS.

–GALATIANS 6:10

No one has ever seen God; but if we love one another, God lives in us and his love is made complete in us.

-1 JOHN 4:12

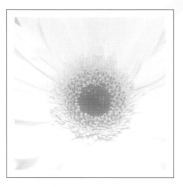

KIND LOVE

It was an unusually hot, muggy, Seattle morning in August, and I was parked at the kitchen table in front of my laptop computer when Les quietly slipped in and set up a fan to cool the room. "I don't know if it will make any difference," Les said, trying to place the fan in just the right place, "but I thought it was worth a try." I don't know if the fan really did anything, but I do recall feeling suddenly soothed by my husband's kindness. Kindness is love's readiness to enhance the life of another person.

—LESLIE PARROTT

Love is kind.

-1 Corinthians 13:4

Lord, help each of us to express love and companionship toward the other in ways that are meaningful. And thank you for the joy and comfort of friendship within our marriage. Amen.

A Kind Word

A kindly word and a tender tone—
To only God is their virtue known;
They can lift from the dust the abject head,
They can turn a foe to a friend instead;
The heart close-barred with passion and pride
Will fling at their knock its portal wide;
What ice-bound barriers have been broken,
What rivers of love have stirred,
By a word in kindness spoken,
By only a gentle word.

-Author Unknown

DECISIONS

One Fourth of July my wife and I agreed never to make final decisions on matters that affected both of us unless we both agreed. If we don't arrive at unity before the bus gets here, we don't get on it. We've relied on this principle in all sorts of situations. Both of us assume responsibility for sharing our feelings honestly because we know we can't go anywhere until we're in agreement.

What we agreed upon that day has had a powerful impact on our marriage. It has forced us to communicate on deeper levels than I ever thought existed, helping us to gain an understanding of our individual viewpoints. It has forced us to look beneath surface opinions and discover the very root of our own thinking. When we disagree about a situation, our commitment to this principle helps us verbalize our feelings until we understand each other. Years have passed since we made that commitment, and it continues to work far beyond our expectations. (It's been keeping us out of arguments ever since!)

-GARY SMALLEY

Bedroom Sanctuary

In most homes the last room to get special attention is the master bedroom. It's the last place a visitor will ever see, so it's often the last place a couple decorates or cleans up. ... Song of Songs 1:17 gives us a visual picture of a marital sanctuary. Two lovers are walking outdoors, imagining that the "green field" is their bed and the "cedar trees" above are the beams of their house. ... Is there a place like this in your marriage where you can find peace, tranquility and relationship? Perhaps the bedroom should become just that place. Instead of a place to sleep and fold laundry, it can become a place to grow deeper in love.

—Bob and Rosemary Barnes

How beautiful you are, my darling!
Oh, how beautiful!
Your eyes are doves.
How handsome you are, my lover!
Oh, how charming!
And our bed is verdant.
The beams of our house are cedars;
our rafters are firs.

-SONG OF SONGS 1:15-17

Lord, give us the desire to affirm, to apologize, and to be genuinely affectionate with each other on a daily basis. Cause our love for each other to be a reflection of your love for us and may it be a sanctuary from the outside world. Help us to make time every day to connect with you and each other. Amen.

I'll Be Praying for You

Praying together is not easy for us. Oh, we pray as a couple before meals, and we pray together when there is a special need or crisis, but we aren't the kind of couple who kneels beside our bed each night. We might be better persons if we did, but we don't. I suppose we could blame our busy and unpredictable schedules, but the truth is that we just haven't developed the discipline to build a consistent shared prayer time into our lives.

Still, one thing we do every day is pray for each other, whether we are together or in separate cities. We made that commitment on our wedding day, and Leslie had the passage from Philippians 1:3–5 engraved inside my wedding band:
"I thank my God every time I remember you ... I always pray with joy because of your partnership in the gospel from the first day until now. ..."

Sometimes one of us will say to the other, "I'll be praying for you today," but most of the time there is just a quiet assurance that we are lifting each other up in prayer.

-LES AND LESLIE PARROTT

BE DEVOTED TO ONE ANOTHER ...
HONOR ONE ANOTHER ABOVE
YOURSELVES. NEVER BE LACKING IN ZEAL,
BUT KEEP YOUR SPIRITUAL FERVOR, SERVING
THE LORD. BE JOYFUL IN HOPE, PATIENT IN
AFFLICTION, FAITHFUL IN PRAYER.

–ROMANS 12:10–12

I pray that you, being rooted and established in
love, may have power, together with all the saints,
to grasp how wide and long and high and deep is
the love of Christ, and to know this love that sur-
passes knowledge—that you may be filled to the
measure of all the fullness of God.

–EPHESIANS 3:17–19

Dear Father, We pray that you would help each of
us in our daily lives to glorify you and lift you up.
Thank you for giving us each other that we might be
partners together in your service. Please remind us
each day to lift each other up to your throne. Amen.

WHEN DID WE
GET SO DIFFERENT?

There are few things about a marriage that need a conscious choice more than the fact that spouses seem to be so different. The very fact that opposites attract brings an element to the marriage relationship that causes choice—to deal with the differences or let them irritate.

One day, after we returned from our honeymoon, we were folding the laundry together. My wife opened the underwear drawer of my dresser, and I heard her burst out laughing. "This is ridiculous. All your shorts are rolled up in these neat little packets, row after row. I can't believe it."

"What's so funny about that?" I asked. "You want to see something funny, take a look at that disaster where you put your underwear. Everything is jammed in so tightly that nothing else will fit."

Over time I learned that my way isn't the right way; it's just one way. We each must choose to accept our spouses for who they are without ... trying to make them like us.

-BOB BARNES

How do I love thee? Let me count the ways.
I love thee to the depth and breadth and height
My soul can reach, when feeling out of sight
For the ends of Being and ideal Grace.
I love thee to the level of everyday's
Most quiet need, by sun and candle-light.
I love thee freely, as men strive for Right;
I love thee purely, as they turn from Praise.
I love thee with the passion put to use
In my old griefs, and with my childhood's faith.
I love thee with the breath,
Smiles, tears, of all my life!

-ELIZABETH BARRETT BROWNING

Lord, help us to remember all the ways and reasons we fell in love.
Help us to be accepting and loving instead of trying to remake the wonderful creation you blessed us with in each other. Amen.

Long-Term Love

On our national survey of long-term marriages, we found three common strands in those marriages that are alive and healthy.

1. First, the marriage relationship comes before other relationships.
2. Second, both spouses are committed to growing and changing together.
3. Third, they work at staying close.

Love is a delicate balancing act. Some things we can control; other things we juggle. In a high-priority marriage, not only do spouses grow and adapt to each other, they also work at staying close.

-Dave & Claudia Arp

Kisses

Of all the little expressions of love—a box of chocolates, a handwritten poem, or a bouquet of handpicked wildflowers—I think my favorite is a good old-fashioned kiss on the lips.

Did you know the word kiss comes from a pre-historic syllable that is believed to be the sound of kissing? However the word originated and whoever named it really doesn't matter to me. I just know I like kisses. And why shouldn't I? Kisses, according to a Danish saying, are the messengers of love.

-LES & LESLIE PARROTT

Let him kiss me with the kisses of his mouth~
for your love is more delightful than wine.

-Song of Songs 1:2

The sound of a kiss is not so
loud as that of a cannon, but
its echo lasts a great deal longer.

-Oliver Wendell Holmes

Dear Lord and Creator, Thank you for the
wonderful gift of kisses. We praise you for
your creativity and the love you show to us by
giving us each other to enjoy. Amen.

Help from Heaven

It is God's will in every marriage that couples love each other with an absorbing spiritual, emotional, and physical attraction that continues to grow throughout their lifetime together. And it is possible for any Christian couple to develop this love relationship in their marriage because it is in harmony with God's express will. Because he is the one who made us, who conceived the idea of marriage for our blessing, and gave us the potential for love, He is the One who knows best how to build love into marriage.

-Ed Wheat

Every house is built by someone, but God is the builder of everything.

-Hebrews 3:4

Dear Lord, we invite you to be intimately involved in all our efforts to develop the kind of marriage that pleases you. We want to experience the marriage that you planned for us from the beginning, filled with your special love all our days. Amen.

My heart is glad and my tongue rejoices;
    my body also will rest secure . . .
You have made known to me
    the path of life, O LORD;
    you will fill me with joy in your presence,
with eternal pleasures at your right hand.

-PSALM 16:9, 11

In the triangle of love between ourselves, God and other people, is found the secret of existence, and the best foretaste, I suspect, that we can have on earth of what heaven will probably be like.

-SAMUEL M. SHOEMAKER

At First Sight?

Do you remember the first time you ever saw each other?
What attracted you to your mate when you first met?
What do you think attracted your mate to you?
What about your first date? Do you remember the first
time you talked about getting married?

-DAVE & CLAUDIA ARP

ARISE, COME, MY DARLING;
    MY BEAUTIFUL ONE, COME WITH ME.
MY DOVE IN THE CLEFTS OF THE ROCK,
    IN THE HIDING PLACES ON THE
MOUNTAINSIDE,
SHOW ME YOUR FACE,
    LET ME HEAR YOUR VOICE;
FOR YOUR VOICE IS SWEET,
    AND YOUR FACE IS LOVELY. ...
MY LOVER IS MINE AND I AM HIS.

-SONG OF SONGS 2:13-14, 16

*Love, all alike, no season
knows nor clime,
Nor hours, days, months,
which are the rags of time.*

-John Donne

Praise the LORD, O my soul,
and forget not all his benefits …
who crowns you with love and compassion,
who satisfies your desires with good things
so that your youth is renewed like the eagle's.

-Psalm 103:2, 4–5

*Delight yourself in the LORD
and he will give you the desires of your heart.*

-Psalm 37:4

Romantic Ideas

You can get a good buy on Valentine cards on February 15! One year we stocked up and hid them in various places all year long. When either one of us found one, we recycled it and hid it for the other to find.

Make a list of things you appreciate about your mate. Our friend Joe made a list of thirty-one things he appreciated about his wife, Linda. He typed them, cut them up, folded them, put them in capsules, and gave them to Linda with the following prescription: "Take one a day for a month."

Once, on a special promotional offer from a local department store, Dave purchased several small sample bottles of perfumes and lotions. He individually wrapped each one, and each evening he hid one under Claudia's pillow. The first night, she was surprised; the second night, she was more surprised; and the third and fourth nights, she even went to bed earlier!

-Dave & Claudia Arp

Dear Heavenly Father, We praise you for the beautiful gift you have given us in each other. Help us to never forget the deep love we share and remind us to show that love in big and small ways all the years of our life together. Amen.

Place me like a seal over your heart,
    like a seal on your arm;
for love is as strong as death,
    its jealousy unyielding as the grave.
It burns like blazing fire,
    like a mighty flame.
Many waters cannot quench love;
    rivers cannot wash it away.
If one were to give
    all the wealth of his house for love,
    it would be utterly scorned.

-SONG OF SONGS 8:6–7

I belong to my lover,
        and his desire is for me.
Come, my lover, let us go to the countryside,
        let us spend the night in the villages.
Let us go early to the vineyards
        to see if the vines have budded,
if their blossoms have opened,
        and if the pomegranates are in bloom—
        there I will give you my love.

-SONG OF SONGS 7:10–12

Dear Lord, Thank you for the life you have given us to spend together. Open our eyes to the opportunities you give us for getting to know each other better and for enjoying our love. Amen.

Best Friends

Blessed is the one who married a best friend. After years and years together, the ultimate compliment silver-haired lovers smile upon each other is: "We are best friends." We may no longer play the same sports or enjoy the same hobbies, but we do delight in each other's company. We love being able to call across the house and know that special person is there—that we can be ourselves and not have to make any kind of impression because our partner accepts us for who we are as a whole. We can sit together without having to make conversation. We can sing or dance together when we are tone deaf and have no sense of rhythm—and even make up our own words if we forget the right ones! That's friendship, that's love—that's life's gift to the soul.

-Pat Matuszak

I want to be your friend

    Forever and ever without break or decay.

When the hills are all flat

    And the rivers are all dry,

When it lightens and thunders in winter,

    When it rains and snows in summer,

When Heaven and Earth mingle—

    Not till then will I part from you.

                -ANONYMOUS

This is my lover,

        this my friend.

                -SONG OF SONGS 5:16

Night and Day

Opposites do attract. To build a strong marriage we must learn how to benefit from the ways we are alike and the ways we are different.

By understanding yourself and your mate, you will be able to balance or compensate.

Our goal in marriage is not to be the same; we are very different. But we need to accept each other and benefit from our differing strengths and accept each other's differing weaknesses.

-Dave & Claudia Arp

*Lord, help us to delight in and
take strength from our differences.
Show us how to be accepting of
each other and live with open
arms for each other. Amen.*

MYSTERIOUS IS THE FUSION OF TWO
LIVING SPIRITS: EACH TAKES THE BEST
FROM THE OTHER, BUT ONLY TO GIVE
IT BACK AGAIN ENRICHED WITH LOVE.

–ROMAIN ROLLAND

Sparking Love

There are endless ways to keep the spark of romance burning brightly in your marriage. While you may want to do a special production now and then, it's the little things that really matter. Little things like coming home early and taking your wife out to dinner at a place she really likes (not the Colonel). Like sending her a note—handwritten—that says, "I want you to know how much I care. I want you to know how much I appreciate all you do. I'm so proud of you."

And, of course, the notes can also flow in the other direction—from wife to husband. Don't forget that one of a husband's basic needs is admiration and respect. You'll never know how many points you can put in his Love Bank by slipping a note into his lunch or jacket pocket that says, "You're such a wonderful husband. I am so lucky you belong to me."

-KEVIN LEMAN

A longing fulfilled is sweet to the soul.

-PROVERBS 13:19

No Such Accident

Marriage doesn't just happen! It takes a solid set of decisions, a huge amount of skill, and enormous willpower. I contend that people in extremely healthy marriages built those marriages just as you build a mammoth bridge or skyscraper. They made their marriage triumphant because they simply wouldn't settle for less.

-Neil Clark Warren

My wife agrees that an intimate sharing time with me is the one thing she enjoys most about our relationship. We make it a point to have breakfast together as often as possible at a nearby restaurant just to talk about our upcoming schedules. I ask her questions about what she needs for the week and what I can do to help her and vice versa. I enjoy our discussions because I know she enjoys them. But more importantly, I would really miss those times of intimate communication if we ever neglected them.

-Gary Smalley

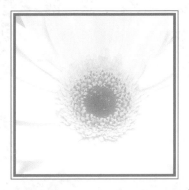

Your inner self, the unfading beauty of a gentle and quiet spirit, … is of great worth in God's sight.

-1 PETER 3:4

A man will leave his father and mother and be united to his wife, and the two will become one flesh.

-EPHESIANS 5:31

MAY YOUR FOUNTAIN BE BLESSED, AND MAY YOU REJOICE IN THE WIFE OF YOUR YOUTH.

-PROVERBS 5:18

REACHING OUT AS A COUPLE

We believe that our shared life must have a sacrificial quality, which leads to service. First we try to serve each other. Then we try to serve others. Marriages can be revolutionized by having a servant's heart.

When we acknowledge that our life together is a part of the divine purpose, we look for ways to live that out in service to others. We believe service promotes spiritual intimacy in a marriage relationship. Can you think of ways that together you can serve others? Maybe you are concerned about ecology and taking better care of our world. Or perhaps you would like to help Habitat for Humanity build houses for people who need a place to live. Your own place of worship offers many opportunities for service. For those who desire to serve, you don't have to look very far to find those who desperately need your help! Every time we get involved in serving others together, our own marriage seems to benefit.

-DAVE & CLAUDIA ARP

Dear Father, open our eyes to ways we can serve you. Help our hearts be tender to the needs of others and thirsty to fellowship with your people. Amen.

Whatever you do, work at it with all your heart, as working for the Lord, not for men, since you know that you will receive an inheritance from the Lord as a reward. It is the Lord Christ you are serving.

-COLOSSIANS 3:23–24

A DAY WELL SPENT

If we sit down at set of sun
And count the acts that we have done,
　　And counting, find
One self-denying act, one word
That eased the heart of him who heard
　　One glance most kind
That fell like sunshine where it went
Then we may count that day well spent.

-AUTHOR UNKNOWN

Home Sweet Home

Years ago we moved into a new house built in an old Seattle neighborhood. The day Brian, our contractor, finally handed us the keys and climbed into his pickup to leave, he asked, "How long will it take you to make this house a home?"

We never really came to a conclusion that day, but we thought about it, off and on, for years. Over time we decided that our house feels most like a home when we put into practice God's principles for loving each other within it. And we've learned in the last few years that the best way to do that is to focus on being a loving person. Surprisingly, that doesn't necessarily mean doing loving things but instead focusing on cultivating a loving attitude by spending time with Jesus. Often, the most loving thing we can do is to sit at Jesus' feet together as husband and wife. When we concentrate on God together, the to-do list falls to the wayside, our priorities get straightened out, and we focus on the really important thing—loving God and each other. No doubt about it—that's when our house is most like a home.

-Les & Leslie Parrott

Father, we want our marriage to be engulfed by love—
your love. And we know that the best way to make
that happen is to spend time together, not doing, but
being in your presence. Teach us to rest in you. Help us
make our home everything you want it to be. Amen.

Jesus said, "If anyone loves me, he
will obey my teaching. My Father
will love him, and we will come to
him and make our home with him."

–John 14:23

As for me and my household, we will serve the Lord.

Joshua 24:15

Pillow Talk

Everyone's best communication time is different, and it may take a blending of schedules to find the best time for you as a couple. Often bedtime is a good time for one spouse, but the worst possible time for the other. When we were first married, Rosemary believed that the time to get involved in deep discussions was when we went to bed. She is a night person. I'm a morning person. Going to bed at the end of the day stimulates Rosemary to talk. Going to bed brings to my mind only two thoughts, and neither of those has to do with in-depth communication!

We would put our heads on the pillow, reach over to turn out the lights, and Rosemary would then launch into some incredible conversation. In seconds I would respond with "Zzzzzz." We quickly realized that our best time for communication was not late at night.

-Bob Barnes

Adam's Song

The world's first love song …

This is now the bone of my bones
and flesh of my flesh;
she shall be called 'woman,'
because she was taken out of man.

-Genesis 2:23

Hebrew experts tell us that Adam was expressing a tremendous excitement, a joyous astonishment. "At last, I have someone corresponding to me!" His phrase, "bone of my bones, and flesh of my flesh," became a favorite Old Testament saying to describe an intimate, personal relationship. But the fullness of its meaning belongs to Adam and his bride. Marriage was planned and decreed to bring happiness.

-Ed Wheat

A Red, Red Rose

O my love's like a red, red rose.
That's newly sprung in June;
O my love's like a melody
That's sweetly played in tune.

As fair art thou, my bonnie lass,
So deep in love am I;
And I will love thee still, my Dear,
Till all the seas run dry.

Till all the seas run dry, my Dear,
And the rocks melt with the sun:
I will love thee still, my Dear,
While the sands of life shall run.

And fare thee well my only Love!
And fare thee well a while!
And I will come again, my Love,
Tho' it were ten thousand mile!

-Robert Burns

A Cord of Three Strands

Our friends Jim and Jeannette wanted something that would express their trust and dependence on God in their marriage, so they came up with what they called the "unity cord."

Standing before the congregation, they braided three cords together, symbolizing the powerful strength of their marriage when they lean not on their own understanding but on the wisdom of God. The three separate cords represented the three participants in this life-long union—Jim, Jeannette, and God's son, Jesus Christ. By the braiding of these three cords Jim and Jeannette visually illustrated their new oneness, intricately interwoven and strengthened by their love of God.

-Les & Leslie Parrot

WHEN WE ACKNOWLEDGE GOD'S PRESENCE IN OUR MARRIAGE, WE ARE INTERTWINING OUR MARRIAGE WITH GOD'S POWER.

Two are better than one,
> because they have a good return for their work:
If one falls down,
> his friend can help him up.
But pity the man who falls
> and has no one to help him up!
Also, if two lie down together, they will keep warm.
> But how can one keep warm alone?
Though one may be overpowered,
> two can defend themselves.
A cord of three strands is not quickly broken.

-ECCLESIASTES 4:9–12

The Goal

My husband, Paul, pounded on the steering wheel in frustration. "Every time I want to go somewhere, I get stuck in this stupid construction traffic. We're going to miss the movie." He wanted to see a movie, so the traffic was blocking his goal. I wanted to have a good time and I didn't care if we went to a movie or Thailand; I was enjoying the conversation.

"Why aren't you having fun?" I asked.

"I'll start having fun when we get there," he answered.

"But I want to have fun on the way, or I won't have fun when we get there," I said.

Some people focus on the destination. Others focus on the journey. Usually God puts one of each in a marriage. Maybe he does that so we don't forget that both are important. Learning to mix the journey and the destination is the secret of the Christian life—setting our sights on heaven and finding joy on earth.

Someone should make a movie about that. I'd go.

-Nicole Johnson

Father, keep us focused on where we're going
and aware of the journey along the way.
Remind us of your love in the process, that we
might find joy in our travels together and hope
in the eternal destination. Amen.

GOOD COMPANY IN A JOURNEY
MAKES THE WAY TO SEEM THE SHORTER.

–IZAAK WALTON

I run in the path of your commands O LORD,
for you have set my heart free.
–PSALM 119:32

LOVE AND LAUGH

The first cousin to encouragement is laughter. There are times in life when you can either laugh or cry. We try to choose laughter. Laughter dispels tension. It's good for your physical health, and it's definitely good for the health of your marriage.

When we laugh together, we seem more affirming. When we're under stress, we benefit from trying to find some way to lighten things up. A couple named Dan and Laura told us a story of how their pets helped relieve tension.

The pressure of school, work, and other responsibilities were taking their toll. After a long day at work, Laura walked into their small apartment and found all three of their cats wearing ties! Dan, in an attempt to make Laura laugh, had tied his ties around the necks of their cats. (It worked.)

-DAVE & CLAUDIA ARP

No Longer Lonely

Marriage was designed by God to meet the first problem of the human race: loneliness.

Picture this one man in a perfect environment, but alone. He had the fellowship of God and the company of birds and animals. He had an interesting job, for he was given the task of observing, categorizing, and naming all living creatures. But he was alone.

God observed that this was "not good." So a wise and loving Creator provided a perfect solution. He made another creature, like the man and yet wondrously unlike him. She was totally suitable for him.

According to God she was designed to be his "helper." This term helper refers to a beneficial relationship where one person aids or supports another person as a friend and ally. Perhaps you have thought of a helper as a subordinate, a kind of glorified servant. You will see the woman's calling in a new light when you realize that the same Hebrew word for help is used of God himself in Psalm 46:1 where he is called our helper, "a very present help in trouble."

-Ed Wheat

The LORD God said, "It is not good for the man to be alone. I will make a helper suitable for him." Now the LORD God had formed out of the ground all the beasts of the field and all the birds of the air. He brought them to the man to see what he would name them; and whatever the man called each living creature, that was its name.

So the man gave names to all the livestock, the birds of the air and all the beasts of the field. But for Adam no suitable helper was found.

So the LORD God caused the man to fall into a deep sleep; and while he was sleeping, he took one of the man's ribs and closed up the place with flesh. Then the LORD God made a woman from the rib he had taken out of the man, and he brought her to the man.

~GENESIS 2:18~22

A Loving Cup

A "Maxwell House moment" is the kind of casual exchange that usually takes place over a cup of coffee. The subject isn't relevant; it's the kind words and the time spent together that matter.

Each of us needs someone to listen to the little everyday aspects of our life.

When you chime in with the occasional "uh huh" or "really?" you're showing that you care not just about the chitchat at hand, but about the speaker, your spouse. And that's good for the soul. It calms our anxious heart and cheers our heavy spirit.

If good everyday communication sounds simple, it is.

What's most important is that you simply have the ability to show love, appreciation, caring, and concern enough to have warm conversations with each other.

-Les & Leslie Parrott

An anxious heart weighs a man down
but a kind word cheers him up.

-PROVERBS 12:25

PLEASANT WORDS ARE A HONEYCOMB, SWEET TO THE SOUL AND HEALING TO THE BONES.

-PROVERBS 16:24

Dear Lord, give us the blessing of an ear to listen to each other and a heart to hear. Amen.

Let your conversation be always full of grace.

-COLOSSIANS 4:6

Discerning God's Will

The major decisions we make in marriage will come more easily if we abide in Christ daily ... seeking to please him. Here are five different means God has given us to help discern his will.

1. The Bible. The single most important question to ask is, "Has God already spoken on this matter?"

2. Prayer. Prayer is the currency of our personal relationship with Christ. Spend it liberally. Pray together over major (why not all?) decisions.

3. The Holy Spirit. The Holy Spirit is the one who "clothes" us with power from on high. The Holy Spirit will never lead in contradiction to his written Word.

4. Conscience. Keep in mind that while a guilty conscience provides clear evidence you are not in God's will, a clear conscience may not guarantee you have correctly discerned God's will. Conscience is more effective as a red light than a green light. To go against conscience is neither wise nor safe.

5. Counsel. Often we need nothing more than a good listener to help us crystallize our thoughts into coherent words. Other times, we need the advice of a trusted friend. Seek out each other's counsel.

-PATRICK MORLEY

Lord, help us always to bring our requests to you, being patient to wait on you as you orchestrate events and circumstances. Remind us not to let go of each other's hand as we pray and wait. Help us to maintain our faith and trust in you. Thank you for hearing us! Amen.

In your unfailing love you will lead
the people you have redeemed, O LORD,
In your strength you will guide them.
-EXODUS 15:13

Trust God for great things; with your five loaves and two fishes, He will show you a way to feed thousands.

-HORACE BUSHNELL

MEMORIES

What do you remember about your wedding day? We reacted totally differently. Claudia was so nervous that she hardly slept the whole night before. Dave took a nap the hour before the ceremony and would have missed the wedding if his dad hadn't awakened him!

Our first home was a tiny basement apartment. We were still in college and had all hand-me-down furniture, including a bed with too-short slats that kept falling in!

It's fun to think back into our history and remember the excitement of that time when we realized we were in love. Memories help us to remember just how important our marriage is and why we want to keep nurturing our relationship. They motivate us today to make our marriage a high priority.

-DAVE & CLAUDIA ARP

JOY THAT LASTS

Most of us need tangible reminders to help us experience God's fullness and remember that he is the source of joy that lasts. Here are a few ideas:

List on three-by-five cards the desires God has given you for loving others. Place each card where you will see it at least once a day; the bathroom mirror, by the phone, on the refrigerator, on the dashboard of your car, or on your office desk.

Buy a special mug to use in the office or your home for coffee breaks. Find one that's painted with a message like "Rejoice in the Lord" or "Love Never Fails." Each time you use it, take a moment to check the contents of your "internal cup."

At dinner, tell what God has done in your lives that day.

Take time to dream together and brainstorm ways to fulfill your mission in life.

-GARY SMALLEY

Taste and see that the Lord is good.

-Psalm 34:8

You ... are being built together to become a dwelling in which God lives by his Spirit.

-Ephesians 2:22

Now to God who is able to do immeasurably more than all we ask or imagine, according to his power that is at work within us, to him be glory.

-Ephesians 3:20-21

THE POWER OF WORDS

Most husbands readily admit they struggle with love. They can't see it, analyze it, or explain it. They often don't feel it, and quite frequently have a hard time expressing it.

Wives crave to hear their husbands express feelings of love in words. Without frequent verbal reassurance, wives can begin to doubt if their husbands even love them at all. He may not sense the same need for verbal affirmations of love as does she. This tends to make him assume she must feel the same way he does.

On the other hand, many husbands do express their love by doing kind things for their wives. Wives need to be more alert to the nonverbal ways in which their husbands do signal their love and affection. Properly understood, these kindnesses can be received by the wife as important deposits into her emotional bank account. By the same token, husbands need to verbally express their love often.

And wives, don't neglect expressing your love through words of appreciation for your husband's hard work for the family. Any words of encouragement mean so much to a man.

-Patrick Morley

Be kind and compassionate to one another.

-EPHESIANS 4:32

Poet to His Love

An old silver church in a forest
Is my love for you.
The trees around it
Are the words that I have stolen from your heart.
An old silver bell, the last smile you gave,
Hangs at the top of my church.
It rings only when you come through the forest
And stand beside it.
And then it has no need for ringing,
For your voice takes its place.

-MAXWELL BODENHEIM

Growing a Marriage

Marriage, like life, is progressive. You can't build a life or a marriage in one day, one week, or one year. As a newlywed couple, God often provides for you through others. For instance, we benefited from those we met along the way. We remember an older couple who befriended us. We were still in college and they generously took us out to eat each Sunday after church. Another time God's provision came through a book that just happened to answer a specific need, and through a sermon that encouraged us.

Being faithful to learn what God wants to teach you will result in more growth in the future. When you invest in your marriage and your walk with God, you will reap great dividends. For instance, developing the habit of regular dates and joining a marriage growth group helped keep our relationship growing.

Growth multiplies as you become more established in your marriage and in your relationship with God. Your roots will draw deeply from God's love, and you can bear much fruit.

The good news is it isn't all up to you. Second Kings 19:31 reminds us, "The zeal of the LORD Almighty will accomplish this."

-DAVID AND CLAUDIA ARP

LET US LEARN TOGETHER
WHAT IS GOOD.
–JOB 34:4

Show me your ways, O LORD,
teach me your paths.
Guide me in your truth
and teach me.

–PSALM 25:4-5

Understanding is a fountain of life
to those who have it.

–PROVERBS 16:22

May the Lord direct your hearts into God's
love and Christ's perseverance.

-2 THESSALONIANS 3:5

Prayer

Prayer is a unique spiritual resource in marriage. For us, praying together promotes spiritual closeness.

At times we take a tip from our Quaker friends and try the Quaker practice of sharing silence. This allows us to worship according to our own personal needs, to seek communion with God separately and privately, yet be supported by the awareness that our spouse is also sharing in the experience. It's an easy first step in praying and worshiping together. According to the Quaker tradition, the devotional time is appropriately concluded with the kiss of peace.

-Dave & Claudia Arp

Feels Like Love

What feels like love varies from person to person—this is why we need to know our mate so well. One person may measure love by the way his material needs are met, or by tangible items such as expensive gifts. Another may feel loved when her husband helps her with the dishes. One will measure love by the amount of time spent together, or by the quality of openness and sharing of thoughts between the two. There are so many languages of love! We need to learn what speaks to our own partner so we can express our love in ways that cannot be doubted. We should also share exactly what it is that makes us feel loved ourselves.

-ED WHEAT

_We_ are each of us
angels with only one
wing. And we can only
fly embracing each other.

–Luciano de Cresenzo

_Lord, sometimes we get caught up in thinking
about how our spouse can meet our needs, but
we forget it is more blessed to give than to
receive. Help us to express love and companionship toward the other in ways that are meaningful. And thank you for the joy of friendship
within our marriage. Amen._

Love Bridges

Walls are everywhere, but so are bridges. Whether you build a wall or a bridge depends upon your purpose. We want to let our mates in. The motivations to build bridges are the desire for intimacy, to give and receive love, and to have a friend. Walls keep us apart; bridges bring us together.

The most important bridge in marriage is communication. Words are the slabs of stone in the stream that get us over to the other side. Listening is the bridge that draws our mate over to us.

A marriage without walls is a marriage with bridges.

-Patrick Morley

Lord Jesus, thank You for building a bridge between us. We want to have a marriage without walls and that is constantly getting better. Show us where the bridges are washed out. Show us where to make repairs. Show us where new bridges need to be built. Amen.

Was it not the LORD who dried up the sea,
the waters of the great deep,
who made a road in the depths of the sea
so that the redeemed might cross over?

-ISAIAH 51:10

That's Funny

Laughter is the shortest distance between two people—especially in marriage. The tiniest things can sometimes set us off—an inflection or a knowing glance, a funny line from a movie, or a faux pas in front of others. We have the same funny bone!

Research has shown that people with a sense of humor have fewer symptoms of illness than those who are less humorous. Perhaps that's what Proverbs 17:22 is getting at.

The benefits of humor extend beyond our physiology. The Bible reminds us many times and in many ways to bring the "sounds of joy and gladness" (Jeremiah 33:11) to our homes. Proverbs says, "The cheerful heart has a continual feast" (Proverbs 15:15). The psalmist sings, "Our mouths were filled with laughter" (Psalms 126:2). Isaiah exults, "Shout for joy, O heavens; rejoice, O earth" (Isaiah 49:13).

-LES & LESLIE PARROTT

A cheerful heart is good medicine.

-PROVERBS 17:22

Dream a Little Dream with Me

Marylyn and I find that dreaming together is very romantic. We actually think that dreaming and envisioning our life are the essence of our romance. We're convinced that any couple who dreams about their future together is bound to fall in love over and over and over. Nothing in the world is as attractive as someone who will dream with you, merge their dreams with yours, clarify the path toward the realization of those dreams, and lock their arms into yours while walking down the path.

At the center of all this dreaming and planning is a certain theme: "I want the future to be good for you. If it isn't good for you, it can't be good for us."

Being cared for this way is the core of romance. We've been married for a long time and we know if we will keep our marital dream alive it will fill our marriage with energy. It sets us free to know the joy that comes from moving forward through life with the person we love. When we work out our dreams our hearts are welded together.

-Neil Clark Warren

Dear Father, you are the one who has called us together. Your Spirit gives life and power. Help us to dream a dream for our marriage that has your Spirit at the center. Amen.

THERE'S NOTHING HALF SO
SWEET IN LIFE
AS LOVE'S YOUNG DREAM.

–THOMAS MOORE

"For I know the plans I have for you," declares the LORD, "plans to prosper you and not to harm you, plans to give you hope and a future."

–JEREMIAH 29:11

Pray Together, Stay Together

Couples who frequently pray together are twice as likely as those who pray less often to describe their marriages as being highly romantic. Spiritual intimacy can enhance the overall quality of a marriage.
It's having a shared purpose in life—a calling to something bigger than the two of us. It's our spiritual unity that sees us through life's storms and gives us inner peace in the midst of a turbulent world.

Marriage offers a unique opportunity for this type of intimacy. It provides the time and opportunity for growing together spiritually. When we use the two words together, "spiritual intimacy" means emotional closeness with our Creator, God. And our experience has been that emotional closeness with God contributes to emotional closeness with each other.

-Dave & Claudia Arp

I'll Remember You Love, in My Prayers

When the curtains of night are pinned back by the stars
And the beautiful moon leaps the skies,
And the dewdrops from heaven are kissing the rose,
It is then that my memory flies,
As if on the wings of some beautiful dove
In haste with the message it bears,
To bring you a word of affection and say:
I'll remember you, love, in my prayers.

When heavenly angels are guarding the good
As God has ordained them to do,
In answer to prayers I have offered to Him,
I know there is One watching you.

-Author Unknown

Daily Days

Research reveals that the happiest couples are those who share the mundane details of their days. Most of the time our lives are filled with the unremarkable. To feel connected with one another, it is mandatory to share small details. We need a listening ear for the small triumphs and frustrations of daily living. Listening and sharing with one another is a choice. We carve out time each day to participate in each other's lives and are available to share and actively listen. It helps us feel connected.

-Bob & Rosemary Barnes

I HAVE YOU IN MY HEART; FOR ... YOU
SHARE IN GOD'S GRACE WITH ME.
–Philippians 1:7

It was good of you to share in my troubles.

-Philippians 4:14

Words, Words, Words

Words are the window into the soul. We use words to paint the portrait of our love for each other. "I love the way you do your hair." A few sincere words skillfully clumped together can lift the spirit of your partner high into the heavens. Words are beautiful.

Mark Twain said, "A powerful agent is the right word. The difference between the right word and the almost right word is the difference between lightning and the lightning bug."

There are times when we groan inwardly but the right words will not come. When this happens, we can still communicate by:

*Expressing what we can and let our spouse know we have deeper feeling we can't quite reach at that moment. Our partner will understand and appreciate the effort.

*Asking our mate to help us talk out our feelings

*Doing things that reflect how we feel—if ready to explode with love, we can just give our spouse a hug!

-Patrick Morley

Heavenly Father, thank you for the gift of words and language. Thank you that our language does not always have to be words, but that we can still express ourselves by what we do for each other. Please give us a more intimate relationship through ministering to each other through our words. Amen.

A LOOM

The strength of your love
    weaves music into my soul.
Back and forth, your life is knitting a melody
    only we can hear.

It's a voice without words,
    a whisper that thunders
And calls me by name.

—PAT MATUSZAK

Extra Miles

Love has nothing to lose. It is in the business of giving itself away. Love only has eyes for another person's needs, so in a sense, love can't be robbed. Sure it risks being deceived and hurt, but love's power is found in the very act of taking this vulnerable risk. Love takes an uncalculated chance every time it walks the extra mile. Love doesn't measure the distance beforehand. If love feels a little naive it is not for lack of experience with people, but because love does not bother to calculate what it might lose.

Love's not too careful. Why? Because when love is completely trusting, it is at peace to love all the more.

-Les & Leslie Parrott

This is how God showed his love among us:
He sent his one and only Son into the world
that we might live through him.

-1 JOHN 4:9

❧

LOVE'S GIFT

*L*ove that asketh love again
Finds the barter naught but pain.
Love that giveth in full store
Aye receives as much and more.

*L*ove that asketh nothing back
Never suffers any lack.
Love that seeketh love in pay
Rues the bargain every day.

-DINAH MULOCK CRAIK

A New Name

The nicknames you call each other hold tremendous meaning. "Sweetie," "Honeybun," and even "Spud" are terms of endearment that not everyone feels an inclination to use regarding their spouse, but "Hey you" doesn't hold a candle to "Dimples" —as long as you aren't referring to a cellulite condition!

You have to really be in love to want to be called Mrs. Crabb. But I was eager to assume that new identity from early on in my relationship with Larry. I found the name "Crabb" a most effective one for a schoolteacher. I don't know if the schoolchildren will remember a thing I taught, but I do know they'll remember my name.

The names we call each other contain much power to move us closer together. It's fun to be inventive when we make up endearing names. They can enhance our sense of oneness—even when they are something like "Mrs. Crabb."

-Rachael Crabb

Like a lily among thorns
is my darling among the maidens.
Like an apple tree among the trees of the forest
is my lover among the young men.

-SONG OF SONGS 2:2–3

Dear Lord, thank you for the new names you give to us both in marriage and in spirit. Help us to bestow loving names on each other. We look forward to hearing our names when we see you face to face, when, as your bride, our marriage with you will be celebrated. Amen.

PLEASING IS THE FRAGRANCE OF YOUR PERFUMES;

YOUR NAME IS LIKE PERFUME POURED OUT.

-SONG OF SONGS 1:3

We try to express our feelings for each other with warmth, empathy, and sincerity. Warmth is expressed by communicating a friendly acceptance of the other person. Empathy is the ability to understand and identify with a person's feelings. And sincerity involves being genuinely concerned about a person. Slowly and surely this will open the door for a kind of magic—the power of love—to rekindle our relationship.

—GARY SMALLEY

Lord, help me express myself in such a way that my spouse knows deeply of my love and admiration. Amen.

ALL BEAUTIFUL YOU ARE, MY DARLING;
THERE IS NO FLAW IN YOU.

—SONG OF SONGS 4:7

Love and Forgiveness

We have found that being willing to forgive each other and ask for forgiveness helps to build spiritual intimacy in our relationship. As God forgives us, we can forgive each other. A forgiving spirit helps us to be more compassionate, tolerant, generous, and benevolent with each other. These traits help to build intimacy and trust in marriage.

-Dave & Claudia Arp

Love remains while the world crumbles around her.
While we live here on earth we can only see love in other people,
a very imperfect reflection of the love of Christ, full of faults and
human failures.
But in heaven, we'll see Love in the form of Jesus.
And now I can show love in part—full of my own humanity,
but then I can love perfectly, even as I am completely loved.
The only things that are really important are faith in God, hope
for the future,
and love from God for everyone.
But you cannot have faith or hope
until you first understand and demonstrate love.

-Paraphrase of 1 Corinthians 13 by Angela McCord

Amazing Grace!

The Lord is able to work on our behalf in all circumstances. The hope (better, the certainty) that God is at work to accomplish his plan is rooted in his grace.

When we believe that he is at work and his purposes are always good, then from the depths of our being we will want—really want—to go his way.

Christian marriage counselors usually define love more in terms of actions and decisions than feelings. We know God's love because he did something, not because he felt something. We are often counseled to love our spouses whether we feel like it or not. Our loving actions are not supposed to be led by our erratic emotions, instead we are to follow biblical instruction to loving acts whether our feelings agree or rebel.

While it is true that God displayed his love with unmistakable clarity in what he did; it is equally clear that these actions were accompanied by compassionate emotions. Not only did he do something for us, he also felt something for us. God wants us to share that love he has given us.

-Larry Crabb

To E.

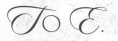

But all remembered beauty is no more
    Than a vague prelude to the thought of you—
You are the rarest soul I ever knew,
    Lover of beauty, knightliest and best;
My thoughts seek you as waves that seek the shore,
    And when I think of you, I am at rest.

-SARA TEASDALE

O God, who has created marriage to represent the spiritual marriage and unity between Christ and his Church; look with mercy on these your servants, that they may love, honor, and cherish each other, and so live together in faithfulness and patience, in wisdom and true godliness, that their home may be a haven of blessing and peace; through the same Jesus Christ our Lord, who lives and reigns with you and the Holy Spirit ever, one God, world without end. Amen.

-Based on the marriage blessing
from The Common Book of Prayer

COVENANT

The commitment we made and accepted in marriage enfolds our whole soul by saying, "I believe in you and commit myself to you through thick and thin." Without commitment and the trust it engenders, marriage would have no hope of enduring. But no couple can achieve deep confidence in the fidelity of themselves and each other until they first recognize God's faithfulness to them.

-LES AND LESLIE PARROTT

BY MAKING A COVENANT WITH US, GOD PROMISED THAT HE IS COMMITTED TO US, AND HE DOES NOT BREAK HIS PROMISES.

-DR. HENRY CLOUD AND DR. JOHN TOWNSEND

"I will never leave you nor forsake you," says the LORD.

~JOSHUA 1:5

The LORD your God is God; he is the faithful God, keeping his covenant of love to a thousand generations of those who love him and keep his commands.

-DEUTERONOMY 7:9

Father, the inspiration that comes from couples who have kept their commitment for so many years is a true blessing. Help us to learn from couples who have lived out their wedding vows. Help us to bring the ideal of commitment down to the daily reality of our lives. And remind us that it is only by your strength that we could ever keep our promise to love our whole lives through. Fill our marriage with the strength of your covenant. Amen.

*Lord, thank you for the gifts
of creativity and humor. Help
us to use both of these qualities
to bring spontaneity, fun, and
memorable moments into our
relationship. Amen.*

The LORD will yet fill your mouth
with laughter
and your lips with shouts of joy.

-JOB 8:21

LAUGH A LITTLE NOW AND THEN
IT BRIGHTENS LIFE A LOT;
YOU CAN SEE THE BRIGHTER SIDE
JUST AS WELL AS NOT.

–AUTHOR UNKNOWN

Romance is Personal

I want to be more romantic. Actually, I want Nicole to think I'm more romantic. The truth is, when you don't really understand what makes something romantic and what doesn't, you can't cultivate it very well. It's a mystery to me. I mean, I can plunk down fifty dollars for a meal and a movie, and on the way home, Nicole tells me she wants more romance. But when I locked the keys in the car, and we had to walk two miles in pouring rain to a pay phone, she told me, "You're so romantic!" That inspired me to lock the keys in the car the next week on purpose; it didn't work like I had hoped. Very confusing.

I have discovered one thing about romance: It must be personal. All the "romance" in the world won't mean a thing to my wife if it doesn't come from me. I know it's strange, but she would rather have my awkward, three-line poem than a beautiful, frilly card quoting Wordsworth.

*R*omance is the electricity around intimacy. Intimacy happens when people give of themselves in a way that is unique and personal. While the Song of Songs depicts what Solomon thinks of love and romance, it also reveals God's longing to relate to us. The Creator of the universe is a personal God. He desires to connect with us intimately. He has reservations for us at places that we enjoy, and he knows our favorite songs. When it came time for him to demonstrate his love, … he carefully crafted what he wanted to say. And he delivered it in the most personal way through Jesus Christ.

-Paul Johnson

You are a garden locked up, my sister, my bride;
      you are a spring enclosed, a sealed fountain.
Your plants are an orchard of pomegranates
      with choice fruits,
      with henna and nard.

-SONG OF SONGS 4:12–13

Lord, give us a true taste of a personal relationship with you so that we might understand how to better love our spouses. We confess in our confusion we often give up and don't love them well at all. Forgive us for the times we've not brought our full hearts to you or to them. Teach us how to love personally. Amen.

A man will leave his father and mother and be united to his wife, and the two will become one flesh. This is a profound mystery—but I am talking about Christ and the church.

-EPHESIANS 5:31–32

Stronger Together

Even after only three years of marriage, my husband and I have discovered how much we complement each other. For example, he has a lot of difficulty remembering names. Many times, as we are on our way to a get-together, he will have me repeat everyone's names so he doesn't embarrass himself once we get there. I call myself his personal walking, talking Rolodex!

On the other hand, he can create a three-page spreadsheet outlining all our expenses with formulas that will add everything up for you at the touch of a button. All I can do is look at it, scratch my head, and thank God for giving me a husband with a head for business!

Because our strengths help compensate for each others' weaknesses we make a strong team. God designed our marriage that way and I'll bet he did the same for you. Have fun exploring each other's strengths. You'll be amazed at how strong you are when you work together the way God designed you to!

-MOLLY DETWEILER

Dear Jesus, Open our eyes each day to the strengths, talents and gifts that you have given us. Show us how to use them to help each other and to strengthen our marriage into a solid partnership. Thank you for the beautiful gift of marriage. Amen.

Jesus said, "[A man and his wife] are no longer two, but one. Therefore what God has joined together, let man not separate."

–Matthew 19:6

1+1=1

Oneness captures in a single, pregnant word the overarching goal of a Christian marriage. Oneness marks the summit of marital union. It is the peak toward which we climb. It is the idea that summarizes scriptural teaching on marriage: "And the two will become one flesh."

Oneness is a state of harmony on which the husband and wife lovingly meet each other's needs and fulfill God's purpose for their marriage. Oneness is to make a third entity of two who forsake themselves for each other. Oneness is symbolized by the formula on my wedding band: "1+1=1." Oneness means that through all we'll be one.

-PATRICK MORLEY

AGAPE

We hear a lot about love, and we all have our own ideas about what love means. To some it is romance, and to others it is security. To still others, it is the feeling of being attracted to some quality that the other possesses, such as power and achievement. We all say, "I love that about you." What we mean when we say this is that there is something in the other person that gratifies us in some way, and we like it. These are all wonderful aspects of loving another person. We celebrate who that person is. He or she adds to our existence. Love is a part of the relationship.

The love that builds a marriage is the kind of love God has for us. It is called "agape." Agape is love that seeks the welfare of the other. It is love that has nothing to do with how someone is gratifying us at the moment. It has to do with what is good for the other. In short, agape is concerned with the good of the other person.

Jesus said it this way in the second greatest commandment: "Love your neighbor as yourself." When we do that, we are truly loving someone.

-DR. HENRY CLOUD AND DR. JOHN TOWNSEND

$\mathcal{M}$ATURE PEOPLE THINK OF NURTURING, DEVELOPING, AND TAKING CARE OF THE TREASURES OF THE PEOPLE WITH WHOM THEY ARE IN RELATIONSHIP.

-DR. HENRY CLOUD AND DR. JOHN TOWNSEND

Love your neighbor as yourself.

-MATTHEW 22:39

$\mathcal{G}$OD $\mathcal{B}$LESS $\mathcal{Y}$OU

I seek in prayerful words, dear friend,
   My heart's true wish to send you;
That you may know that, far and near,
   My loving thoughts attend you.

I cannot find a truer word,
   Nor fonder to caress you.
Nor song nor poem I have heard
   Is sweeter than "God bless you."

-AUTHOR UNKNOWN

Married with Feelings

As newly weds ... you undoubtedly qualify as experts on the feelings of love. ... You know for yourself the euphoric wonder of new love—the magic, the mystery, the miraculous sense of well-being (often described as walking on air) when just being together makes you supremely happy. ...

To preserve your feelings of love, you need clear understanding of them—what they are, essentially; what they can and cannot do; and how to nurture and intensify all the good feelings while you confront the negative ones. ...

Throughout the Bible God reveals a whole tapestry of feelings. The Song of Songs offers a vivid display of feelings of love experienced by a bride and her husband. But nowhere in the New Testament does God ever command us to feel anything. Rather, he would have us to behave in certain ways or to adopt certain attitudes, which will produce certain feelings. It is a principle worth learning that if we obey God with the right actions, the right feelings will soon follow.

-Ed Wheat

*L*OVE MUST BE SINCERE. ... BE DEVOTED TO ONE ANOTHER IN BROTHERLY LOVE. HONOR ONE ANOTHER ABOVE YOURSELVES.

ROMANS 12:9–10

Lord, give us the strength to first allow ourselves to feel, then also to put our mates' needs and feelings above our own. Help us to express our feelings in true love, just as you do toward us each day. Amen.

The Emotional Bank Account

The best way to make your spouse your top priority is to begin thinking in terms of her/his emotional bank account. Learn how your mate likes to give and receive deposits. It may be touching, companionship, support, conversation, small kindnesses, or sex. Your spouse has to bank somewhere; it may as well be with you.

No matter where your marriage stands today, making each other top priority will make it better. You may not even know your mate's account number. That's okay. Ask and it will be given to you.

-Patrick Morley

YOU HAVE IT IN YOU, IT'S SIMPLY A MATTER OF MAKING A CHOICE TO LOVE EACH OTHER DEEPLY. AND THE REWARDS ... ARE GREAT.

–Les and Leslie Parrott

*Lord, keep us from being overdrawn on our
emotional bank accounts with each other.
Help us to make deposits by remembering to
do the little things that say "I love you." Give
us the desire to build up our love account to
overflowing. And remind us that it is your
love within us that enables us to set aside our
selfish desires and love each other the way
we really want to. Amen.*

Give as you would if an angel
    Awaited your gift at the door.
Give as you would if tomorrow
    Found you where giving is o'er.

Give as you would to the Master
    If you met His loving look.
Give as you would of your substance
    If His hand the offering took.

–Author Unknown

A Kiss on the Lips

Soul mates must have integrity. Integrity means telling the truth, keeping our promises, doing what we said we would do, choosing to be accountable, and taking as our motto "semper fidelis"—the promise to be always faithful.

Honesty, as a popular song says, is such a lonely word. At times it does seem that everyone is so untrue. The gift of integrity is so rare. But doesn't your marriage deserve it? So kiss your spouse on the lips with honesty. He or she will say with the psalmist, "The law from your mouth is more precious to me than thousands of pieces of silver and gold" (Psalm 119:72).

-Les and Leslie Parrott

An honest answer is like a kiss on the lips.

-PROVERBS 24:26

FOR TRUTH MAKES HOLY LOVE'S
ILLUSIVE DREAMS,
AND THEIR BEST PROMISE
CONSTANTLY REDEEMS.

–HENRY THEODORE TUCKERMAN

*Speaking the truth in love, we will
in all things grow up into him who
is the Head, that is, Christ.*

-EPHESIANS 4:15

Becoming Best Friends

Many of our Christian friends struggled in their marriages. I decided that I should begin praying for couples I knew who were having troubles. The more I thought about it, the more I sensed that no marriage is invulnerable. As my mind wandered over our own thirteen years of marriage, … it dawned on me that Patsy was not my top priority. … I further realized that our relationship was not deep. Before the Lord I repented and asked God to show me what to do. A plan began to take shape. He showed me how to give Patsy my best.

Without announcing my intentions, I started hanging around the dinner table after the kids left to do homework or whatever. I didn't have an agenda. I just wanted to be with Patsy.

For twenty minutes each day I would ask her about her day, her dreams, her hopes, her fears, her doubts, her concerns. I asked her how she felt the children were turning out and how her spiritual walk was going. I wanted to get to know this woman who had knocked me off my feet over a dozen years earlier. She began to thaw toward me, even warm up. I had forgotten how those big fifty-cent-piece-sized eyes could make my heart go faint.

Within a few weeks we were on the road to becoming best friends. I found that when I chose to respect Patsy, make her my top priority, and treat her with courtesy and appreciation our relationship moved from business to personal. Not long after I changed, Patsy gave me a plaque for my desk. It read, "Happiness is being married to your best friend." Thank you, Jesus.

-Patrick Morley

Love and Life

Love is the foundation for marriage: love for God and love for another person. It expresses itself in seeking the best for the other person no matter whether they deserve it or not. It places the other person above one's own selfish needs and desires. It sacrifices, gives, and suffers. It weathers hurts and storms for the long-term preservation of the covenant. It preserves itself as if it is fighting for life. And in the end, that is exactly what is happening, for love and life were meant to be partners from the beginning of creation.

-Dr. Henry Cloud and Dr. John Townsend

HE HAS TAKEN ME TO THE BANQUET HALL,
AND HIS BANNER OVER ME IS LOVE.

–SONG OF SONGS 2:4

*Marriage is not a lifelong attraction of two
individuals to each other but a call for two
people to witness together to God's love. ...
The real mystery of marriage is not that husband and wife love each other so much that
they can find God in each other's lives but
that God loves them so much that they can
discover each other more and more as living
reminders of God's presence. They are
brought together, indeed, as two prayerful
hands extended toward God and forming in
this way a home for God in this world.*

–HENRI NOUWEN

LISTEN TO UNDERSTAND

Francis of Assisi once said, "Lord, let my quest be to understand rather than be understood." Sometimes when couples sit down to talk, one person makes demands while the other person can't even get a word in. We can issue edicts and never listen to try and understand what the other person is saying. Or we can stop, look, and listen. It's only when we stop, look, and listen that we are choosing to understand what our spouses are trying to say.

—BOB AND ROSEMARY BARNES

IF WE CAN SLOW OUR WORDS AND REACTIONS, PERHAPS WE COULD BE BETTER LISTENERS. BUT DON'T JUST LISTEN FOR THE WORDS—LISTEN FOR THE FEELINGS AS WELL.

—DAVE AND CLAUDIA ARP

COMMUNICATION IS NOT A MATTER OF
BEING RIGHT BUT OF STARTING A FLOW OF
ENERGY BETWEEN TWO PEOPLE THAT CAN
RESULT IN MUTUAL UNDERSTANDING.

–JOHN A. SANFORD

*Everyone should be quick
to listen, slow to speak and
slow to become angry.*

–JAMES 1:19

*I enjoy being with her, looking at her, walking with
her, and talking to her.*

–HUSBAND MARRIED FOR NINETEEN YEARS

Learn how to talk about those things that
really matter to you. Communication and
intimacy grow a love relationship.

–WIFE MARRIED FOR FORTY-SEVEN YEARS

Make Time for Love

When your marriage comes first, everything else falls into its proper place. I realize this may be a strange idea for many wives and husbands. The hard-driving husband who is out there "breaking his neck for his wife and the kids" working sixty or seventy hours a week may find it just too hard to swallow. And it may seem impossible to a mom with three little ankle-biters who consume her twenty-four hours a day. Just where is she supposed to find all this time for her husband (assuming he's even around)?

Nonetheless, I stand by my top priority. For any couple—particularly the overly busy, hard-driving husbands and wives who are trying to juggle career and family—there are plenty of reasons to seek refuge in each other, to have some time for yourselves. Finding time for each other can be done—if you both really want to.

—Dr. Kevin Leman

Lord, life pulls at us from so many different directions. In the vortex of all the activity, give us creative ways to find rest with one another. Help us to hold onto each other rather than push each other away when too many demands call for our attention. Amen.

The LORD says, "My Presence will go with you, and I will give you rest."

-Exodus 33:14

MARRIAGES MAY BE MADE IN HEAVEN BUT PEOPLE ARE RESPONSIBLE FOR THE MAINTENANCE WORK.

-FROM *CHANGING TIMES*

Building Marriage around the Bible

Each marriage selects, knowingly or not, a moral centerpiece around which it builds. The Bible is the most sensible, practical, and promising centerpiece around which to build a romantic, fulfilling marriage.

Because the Bible is true, it has authority and power. It accomplishes its intended purpose. Personally, I have never known anyone whose life has changed in any significant way apart from the regular study of God's Word. The greatest potential for meaningful change in our marriages is to submit to the authority of God's Word and regular study. When once our souls begin to fill up with the beauty of God's own words, we come into possession of life transforming power.

The Bible is true, practical, and it changes lives. What better basis upon which to build an intimate, loving, open, honest marriage? Wise is the couple that builds their marriage upon the Bible.

-Patrick Morley

*Your word, O Lord, is a lamp to my feet
and a light for my path.*

-Psalm 119:105

Dear God, by faith we accept the Bible as your inerrant Word. We believe it is true. We surrender our own best thinking to the moral authority of your Word. We commit ourselves to regularly study the Bible. Let your Word accomplish in our lives whatever you desire—"the purpose for which you sent it." Amen.

The ever-living Christ is here to bless you. The nearer you keep him, the nearer you will be to one another.

–Geoffery Francis Fisher

Friends Are Loyal and Helpful

Loyalty in marriage means that you let the small things go by. Loyalty means that you don't correct your teammate in public. When your spouse is getting all the attention being loyal means that you stand back and cheer rather than interrupt or get jealous. ...

A friend senses a need and takes on the difficult jobs. It's one thing to respond pleasantly when asked for help, but it's an even greater friend who sees a need and goes after the job without being asked for help. That's when being a friend is all about. ... As marriage partners, ... we must focus on being a friend to our partners. Because friends can't relax until their best friend can relax with them.

—BOB AND ROSEMARY BARNES

THE POWER OF LOVE

Two people falling in love is a powerful emotional event. That it happens to both lovers at the same time intensifies the sense of delight. There is a thrill of newness and a sense of wonder as if the two lovers have entered into a new reality—almost like time-space travel—in which they see themselves and their old world in a different light. C. S. Lewis said, in describing his relationship with his wife Joy, that even his body "had such a different importance" because it was the body his wife loved!

The term falling accurately depicts the suddenness and drama of the situation. The phrase in love correctly implies that the lovers are no longer where they were. They have left themselves as individuals to dwell in a new place together—"a sage and intimate world."

Four significant things usually occur when love is genuine:
The lovers long to be together.
The lovers see each other in a unique way.
The lovers desire to commit themselves to one another.
The lovers want to marry, to be together "forever."

The principles involved in falling in love can help any couple stay in love and grow in love … during the course of a full and happy marriage. All the enjoyable emotions will be there, even the sense of fresh wonder, of seeing each other and life itself through love-washed eyes.

-ED WHEAT

"*I* have loved you with an
everlasting love;
    I have drawn you with loving-
kindness," says the LORD.

-JEREMIAH 31:3

I will search for the one my heart loves. . . .
    When I found the one my heart loves.
I held him and would not let him go.

-SONG OF SONGS 3:2, 4

*How beautiful you are and how pleasing,
O love, with your delights!*

-Song of Songs 7:6

Sources

Arp, David and Claudia. *10 Great Dates*. Grand Rapids: ZondervanPublishingHouse, 1997.

Barnes, Robert and Rosemary. *Rock-Solid Marriage*. Grand Rapids: ZondervanPublishingHouse, 1994.

Barnes, Robert and Rosemary, et al. *The Marriage Devotional Bible*. Grand Rapids: ZondervanPublishingHouse, 2000.

Crabb, Larry, et al. *Bring Home the Joy*. Grand Rapids: ZondervanPublishingHouse, 1998. *The Marriage Builder*. Grand Rapids: ZondervanPublishingHouse, 1992. *Men & Women: Enjoying the Differences*. Grand Rapids: ZondervanPublishingHouse, 1993.

Crabb, Rachael and Larry, et al. *Joy Breaks for Couples*. Grand Rapids: ZondervanPublishingHouse, 2000.

Leman, Kevin. *Keeping Your Family Together When the World Is Falling Apart*. New York. Delacort, 1992.

Morley, Patrick. *Devotions for Couples*. Grand Rapids: ZondervanPublishingHouse, 1994.

Parrott, Les and Leslie. *Love Is....* Grand Rapids: ZondervanPublishingHouse, 1999. *Like A Kiss on the Lips*. Grand Rapids: ZondervanPublishingHouse, 1997.

Smalley, Gary. *Joy that Lasts*. Grand Rapids: ZondervanPublishingHouse, 1988. *For Better or For Best*. Grand Rapids: ZondervanPublishingHouse, 1988. *Hidden Keys of a Loving, Lasting Marriage*. Grand Rapids: ZondervanPublishingHouse, 1988.

Walsh, Sheila. *Faith, Hope, and Love*. Grand Rapids: ZondervanPublishingHouse, 1998

Warren, Neil Clark. *Learning to Live with the Love of Your Life and Loving It!* by Neil Clark Warren, Ph.D. (formerly published under the title *The Triumphant Marriage*,) a Focus on the Family book published by Tyndale House. Copyright © 1995 by Neil Clark Warren, Ph.D.

Wheat, Ed. *Love Life for Every Married Couple*. Grand Rapids: ZondervanPublishingHouse, 1980.